The Silliest
EASTER
JOKE BOOK
FOR KIDS AND FAMILY

RIDDLELAND

INTRODUCTION

What is your favorite part about Easter? Dyeing eggs? Making baskets? Hunting what the Easter Bunny left for you? Donning new clothes? Attending worship? Having a family feast? Eating a chocolate rabbit? Something else?

No matter how you and your family celebrate Easter, the chances are that somebody is going to crack a good Easter-related joke. That person can be you.

Jokes liven up an event; jokes make an event memorable. In fact, some jokes are the highlight of the day, and family members share them year after year after that.

In this book, you will find 300+ jokes. They are not only good jokes; they are jokes with an Easter theme. The jokes in this book are original in the sense that they were not copied from other joke books, and they have been framed in a unique way, but the punchlines are very common in society. By memorizing your favorites, you'll be ready to pop off with a joke whenever the opportunity arises. Inside this book, you'll find question-and-answer jokes, puns, and knock-knock jokes, all with Easter themes.

You'll want to read this book cover to cover; you don't want to miss a thing. But, if you are in a hurry, the question-and-answer/punny jokes are categorized for your convenience, so you can go immediately to the subject matter that interests you at the moment. The book is broken into six chapters: question-and-answer jokes, punny jokes, and knock-knock jokes. They cover the topics of chickens, the Easter bunny, chocolate bunnies, hot-cross buns, jelly beans, Easter baskets, and more. Now, as the Easter Bunny would say, "Let's hop to it and start reading."

TABLE OF CONTENTS

Introduction ~~~~~~~~~~~~~~~~~~~~~ **pg.3**

Chapter 1:
Chickens, Hens and Roosters ~~~~~~~~~ **pg.5**

Chapter 2:
The Easter Bunny and his Bunny
Friends ~~~~~~~~~~~~~~~~~~~~~~~~~ **pg.22**

Chapter 3:
Chocolate Bunnies, Easter Lilies and
Easter Eggs ~~~~~~~~~~~~~~~~~~~~~ **pg.53**

Chapter 4:
Hot-Cross Buns and Jelly Beans ~~~~~~ **pg.69**

Chapter 5:
Easter Baskets, Lent, and Plastic Grass ~ **pg.77**

Chapter 6:
Easter Knock-Knock Jokes ~~~~~~~~~~ **pg.87**

Did You Enjoy The Book? ~~~~~~~~~~ **pg.99**

About Riddleland ~~~~~~~~~~~~~~~~ **pg.100**

CHAPTER 1

CHICKENS, HENS AND ROOSTERS

Question-and-Answer Jokes are probably the most common jokes kids tell. The joke teller asks a simple question, but the response that is expected in return is far from the serious response one would expect. In many cases, the response has a double meaning. What makes these punny ones funny is that one is not quite sure what the person meant to say. For instance, in the first joke, "cheep" can be the sound chickens make, but it sounds just like "cheap," meaning at low cost.

Meanwhile, in the second joke, "fowl" can mean birds, but it sounds just like "foul," which means vulgar and unacceptable. Words that sound the same but are spelled differently are called homophones. As you might suspect, one of the two meanings is often missed by the casual listener.

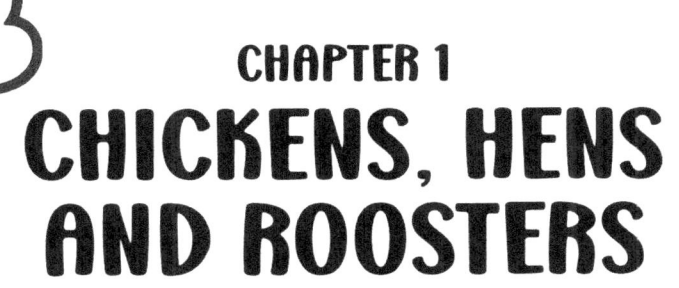

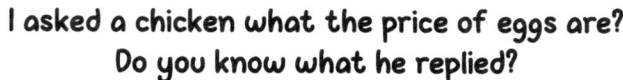

I asked a chicken what the price of eggs are?
Do you know what he replied?

"Cheep! Cheep!"

Why should you avoid words like "geese,"
"chicken," "turkey," and "hen" around my mom?

She doesn't like to hear fowl words.

Which animal gives birth
to psychics?

The chicken; it lays medium eggs.

Why was the hen worried
when the Easter Bunny walked in front of her?

She was a hare behind where she wanted to be.

How is a henhouse like an onion?

It has many layers inside it.

Which direction does
the Easter Hen move to lay her eggs?

Cluck-wise.

What do you call a person
who raises chickens?

A chicken tender.

What type of movie
do egg-laying hens enjoy?

A good chick flick.

What does the chicken do when she needs
to do something she doesn't know how to do?

She wings it.

Who is the chicken's favorite
classical composer?

"Bach! Bach! Bach!"

Why did the chicken study
before trying to lay an Easter egg?

She wanted Grade A eggs.

Why couldn't the
Easter Chicken locate her eggs?

She mislaid them.

What happened when
the chickens got bored with laying eggs?

They wanted to fly the coop.

Which social media platform
do chickens use?

Face bawk.

What does the chicken
call his backpack?

"A bok-bok."

Why aren't
most chickens creative?

They don't think outside the bawks.

**What dessert
do chickens like?**

Coop cakes.

**What kind of products
do chickens ask for by name?**

Cheap.

**Why do chickens
sit on eggs?**

They can't find chairs.

**How do hens dip
their eggs in dye?**

In one fowl swoop.

**What did the hen
say to the bully rooster?**

"Peck on someone your own size."

**What kind of outing
does the Easter chicken enjoy?**

A peck-nic.

Why are chicken coops
such complex places?

They have many layers.

Which muscles do
chickens work on at the gym?

Their pecks.

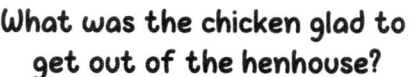

What was the chicken glad to get out of the henhouse?

It was feeling cooped up.

Which animal can pilot farm buildings?

The chicken can fly the coop.

Why was the momma hen sad?

Her son wasn't being all she thought he was cracked up to be.

Why are actions more important to chickens than words?

Talk is cheap.

Which is the smelliest farm animal?

The chickens emit a fowl odor.

What did the chicken do when the farmer fed it and gave it a survey?

Gave him some feedback.

Why was the newborn chick
so nervous?

She had shellshock.

Did you see the relay race?

The Easter Bunny took all the hens' eggs, and the hens had to re-lay more.

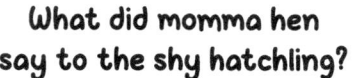

What did momma hen
say to the shy hatchling?

"Come out of your shell."

How is the Easter hen
able to lay all those eggs?

Hen-durance.

How much does a hen
charge for each egg?

A bach.

Do chickens always give up
their eggs willingly?

No. Sometimes, you have to ruffle some feathers.

What plant produces
the most chickens?

The eggplant.

What do you call the hens
that lay the Easter eggs?

Spring chickens.

What did the demon-possessed chicken
offer the Easter Bunny?

Deviled eggs.

What did the chicken
say on payday?

"Buck! Buck! Buck!"

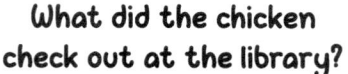

What did the chicken
check out at the library?

"Book! Book! Book! Book!"

What did the chicken say
when the farmer stood too close?

"Back! Back! Back! Back!"

What did the chicken say when the pitcher started
to throw the baseball but didn't do it?"

"Balk! Balk! Balk! Balk!"

How can the Easter Bunny afford
to give away all those eggs?

His hens work for chicken feed.

Why were the hen's eggs
triangular instead of oval?

She mislaid them.

How do chickens
encourage each other?

They egg each other on.

What do chickens
say to start a race?

"Last one there is a rotten egg."

What did the pessimistic rooster crow
at the start of the day?

"Cockadoodle-don't."

Why is the chicken willing to take the blame
if the Easter eggs aren't perfect?

"Because the buck-buck-buck stops here."

How did the egg-laying
chicken end its work shift?

She clucked out for the day.

How is an egg with a pimple
like a door that leads outside?

One is an "egg zit", and the other is an "exit".

How is an egg starring in a play
like a precise measurement?

One is "egg's act," and the other is "exact".

How is an egg in prison like
a Microsoft computer program that does graphs?

One is "egg's cell", and the other is "Excel".

How is an egg that holds coins
like kids swapping lunches?

One is an "egg's change", and the other is an "exchange".

How is an egg wearing glasses
like an enthusiastic cheerleader?

One is "egg sighted", and the other is "excited".

How is an egg in armor
like a match lighting dynamite?

One is "egg knight", and the other is "ignite".

How is an egg writing C-A-T on the white board like a teacher asking the naughty boy to go to the principal's office?

One is "eggs spell," and the other is "expel".

How is a terrible odor
from an egg like a dinosaur?

One is "egg stink", and the other is "extinct".

How is a river with eggs floating in it
like receiving a grade of A++?

One is "egg stream," and the other is "extreme."

How is an egg on a private island
like a person who is banned from the tribe?

One is "egg's isle," and the other is "exile".

How are two eggs resting
on a bench like a fire escape?

One is an "eggs sit", and the other is an "exit".

How are eggs on a plate
with a slice of ham like a test?

One is an "eggs-ham" combination, and the other is an "exam."

How are eggs an artist is drawing,
like a picture of x-ray film that has seen light?

One is "eggs posed," and the other is "exposed."

How are eggs on a plate
with a leaf of spearmint like a science project?

One is "eggs-spearmint," and the other is "experiment".

CHAPTER 2
THE EASTER BUNNY AND HIS BUNNY FRIENDS

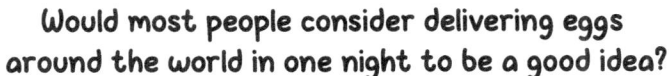

Would most people consider delivering eggs
around the world in one night to be a good idea?

No, it's a hare-brained idea.

Where does the Easter Bunny
prefer to store his sugar?

In suites.

How is the Easter Bunny
like a brewery?

Both specialize in hops.

Where does the Easter Bunny
stay while on vacation?

At a Hare B&B.

What is the Easter Bunny's
philosophy of life?

"Don't worry; be hoppy."

Why do employees tread so carefully
at the Easter Bunny's manufacturing plant?

They have to walk on eggshells.

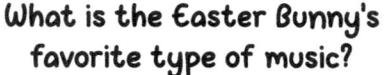

What is the Easter Bunny's favorite type of music?

Hare metal.

What does the Easter Bunny do when something needs to be done in a hurry?

He hops to it.

What happened when the Easter Bunny found a library book about egg dyeing?

He checked it out.

What does the Easter Bunny use to find his misplaced keys?

A hare-tag.

In what school subject do rabbits excel?

Math: rabbits are known for multiplying.

What kind of rabbit lives in your nose?

Nose hares.

What happened when the Easter Bunny
got in trouble for littering?

He had a warren out for his arrest.

Was the result close when the rabbit
and the tortoise had a rematch?

I'm not sure; I heard the race was won by a hare.

How does the Easter Bunny call a meeting to order
when he needs to make a big announcement?

"Hare ye, hare ye . . ."

What do you call the Easter Bunny's cousin
who administers laughing gas to dental patients?

The Ether Bunny.

How did the Easter Bunny
do on his overnight hike?

He was a hoppy camper.

Do you know what it means
when the hens lay the eggs, and the rabbits inspect them?

Every bunny's a critic.

Why did the cash-strapped Easter Bunny
offer a dating site to his egg-providing friends?

He wanted to make hens meet.

Why is the Easter Bunny worried
that his workers are going to mutiny?

He heard the hens discussing a coup.

What's the Easter Bunny's
favorite part of a car?

The eggs-cellerator.

How does the Easter Bunny get all those eggs
delivered in one night; is it luck or skill?

I vote luck; he's got four lucky rabbit's feet.

Is the Easter Bunny nervous?

He's a little jumpy.

Does the Easter Bunny pay the hens
that lay the Easter eggs?

I heard the hens get chicken feed.

What did the Easter Bunny specialize in
when he went to college?

Egg-onomics.

How did the Easter Bunny color
his fur bright orange?

With hare spray.

Why was the girl upset when
the Easter Bunny sipped her milk?

She didn't like seeing a hare in her milk.

Is the Easter Bunny's
factory a busy place?

The employees are definitely hopping.

How does the Easter Bunny
comb his fur?

With a hare brush.

What does the Easter Bunny
use if his fur gets wet in the rain?

A hare dryer.

Are the Easter Bunny's
ears healthy?

They are a sound organ.

How is a row of Easter Bunny-shaped flower pots
with seeds like a balding man?

One is a re-seeding hare line, and the other is a receding hairline.

Where does the Easter Rabbit
like to practice skiing?

The bunny hill.

What did the Easter Bunny
want on Valentine's Day?

Some bunny to love.

Where does
the Easter Bunny live?

In his natural rabbitat.

What kind of dog does
the Easter Bunny own?

A basket hound.

What did the Easter Bunny do while he was employed at the beauty salon?

Dye jobs.

How is the Easter Rabbit wearing his hair this year?

In a bun.

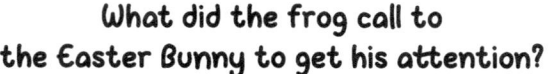

What did the frog call to
the Easter Bunny to get his attention?

"Rabbit. Rabbit."

What happened when
the Easter Bunny learned to speak "frog"?

He became a bunny ribbit.

How can you tell if a rabbit burrow
is full of senior adults?

If you look closely, you'll notice some grey hares.

What's the Easter Bunny's
favorite party game?

Musical Hares.

What does the Easter Bunny
say at the start of a cheer?

"Hip hop . . . hooray!"

Why can't you believe
what the Easter Bunny tells you?

Because it's hare-say.

What does the Easter Bunny
become if he has to work outdoors in the high heat?

A hot cross bun.

Why couldn't all the rabbits
fit in the cage?

The cage was a hare too small.

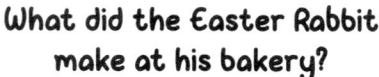

**What did the Easter Rabbit
make at his bakery?**

Something bunny.

**How is letting the Easter Bunny step
into line in front of you like going to the barber for a trim?**

Both are hare cuts.

**Why do people dress up
as the Easter Bunny?**

Because to hare is human.

**What was the Easter Bunny's
favorite type of stories as a young bun?**

Tales.

**What story interested
the youthful Easter Bunny the most?**

He was fascinated with his cotton tale.

**If the Easter Bunny's tail fell off,
where would he have to go?**

To a re-tail store.

What kind of vehicle does
the Easter Bunny drive at the beach?

A dune bunny.

How is the scope of a camera similar
to two angry bunnies in a burrow?

Both have cross hares.

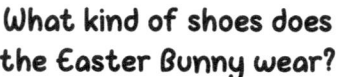

What kind of shoes does
the Easter Bunny wear?

Nike Hare.

What do the barber and the skinned-knee
Easter Bunny have in common?

Hare cuts.

How did the Easter Bunny feel
after finishing his world tour?

He had lots of eggs and pains.

What happened when the boy
was giving rabbits piggyback rides, and his dad said, "Boo."

All the hares on his back stood up.

Do you know why
the Easter Bunny sniffs outdoor air?

He nose.

What did the Easter Bunny, pretending to be a pirate,
tell his crew about the treasure's location?

"Eggs marks the spot."

Did you know that the Easter Bunny
pays his workers with vegetables?

They all work for a celery.

What part of the Easter Bunny
must care be used in describing?

Detail.

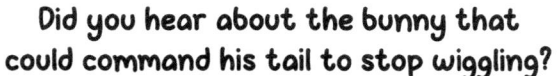

Did you hear about the bunny that
could command his tail to stop wiggling?

It was a tail of whoa.

What is the Easter Bunny's
favorite letter of the alphabet?

It's the 24th letter, eggs.

Is it scary having
baby rabbits as pets?

It's hare-raising.

Why did the Easter Bunny
take his family to the barber shop?

To get hares trimmed.

What was the Easter Bunny having
when his oldest son misbehaved?

A bad hare day.

Where does the Easter Bunny store
his eggs in the Arctic?

In an egg-loo.

Is the Easter Bunny creative
when decorating eggs?

By every sketch of the imagination.

What bunny is even dirtier
than the egg-dyeing Easter Bunny?

The dust bunny.

Why did the Easter Bunny turn
the thermostat in his henhouse to over 212 degrees?

He wanted to see if the hens would lay hard-boiled eggs.

What does classical music have in common with what the
Easter Bunny does with eggs when he visits homes?

Haydin.

Is getting your picture made
with the Easter Bunny scary?

It's hare-riffic.

What did the Easter Bunny's
right ear say to his left ear?

"Between us, something smells."

Why is an Easter Bunny
a rare sight after Easter?

Its eggs stink (extinct).

What did the embarrassed Easter Bunny say
when someone pointed out his messy bookcase?

"I'm ashamed of my shelf."

How does the Easter Bunny
leave a building?

Through the eggs-it.

Why did the Easter Bunny ask
for a stripe to be placed on an egg?

He wanted to draw the line.

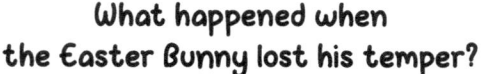

**What happened when
the Easter Bunny lost his temper?**

He was hopping mad.

**Why is the Easter Bunny
so special?**

Because there is no bunny like him.

**How is the Easter Bunny
like a cowboy?**

Both are quick on the draw.

**Was the Easter Bunny okay
with using food coloring as egg dye?**

He found the colors to be palatable.

**The Easter Bunny delivers Easter eggs;
which rabbit delivers jokes?**

The Easter Punny.

**Why does the Easter Bunny's egg
factory show his character?**

Because you can see the Easter Bunny's true colors there.

What kind of shoes does
the Easter Bunny wear when entering homes?

Sneakers.

What can the funny bunny
always deliver?

Laughs.

What kind of stories does the Easter Bunny tell?

Stories with hoppy endings.

Why does the Easter Bunny keep hopping with his basket unless he accidentally drops an egg?

His motto is "Hop 'til you drop."

When the Easter Bunny was in a band, what genre of music did he play?

Hip hop.

Who's going to be egg hunting on Easter?

Any bunny who's any bunny.

How much are the Easter Bunny's two front teeth worth?

They are buck teeth.

What is the Easter Bunny's favorite time of day?

Hoppy hour.

Why did the Easter Bunny
win an award?

He really delivered!

Why is the Easter Bunny so calm?

He boils his eggs so he never has to scramble.

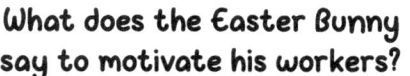

What does the Easter Bunny
say to motivate his workers?

"Hop to it."

What did the Easter Bunny say
when asked why his tale was stubby?

"It may not be much, but I'm attached to it."

What did the Easter Bunny
say about his long-term plans?

"I have lots of hops and dreams."

What does the Easter Bunny do
if he is not paying attention?

"Egg-nore."

What does
the Easter Bunny call a test?

"An eggs-am."

What does the Easter Bunny call a sample?

"An eggs-ample."

What does the Easter Bunny
step on to get his car to go fast?

"The eggs-celerator."

What does an Easter Bunny say
when he doesn't know anything about a subject?

"I am egg-norant about that."

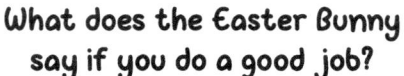

What does the Easter Bunny
say if you do a good job?

"Eggs-cellent."

What kind of work does
the Easter Bunny praise?

"Eggs-ceptional."

If the Easter Bunny wants a change to a norm,
what does he ask for?

"An eggs-ception."

If somebody almost sees
the Easter Bunny as he hides eggs, what does he do?

"Eggs-cape."

How does the Easter Bunny
feel as Easter gets close?

"Eggs-cited."

What does the Easter Bunny
call a tall tale?

"An eggs-aggeration."

What does the Easter Bunny
call a trade?

"An eggs-change?"

Why does the Easter Bunny get along
with everyone so well?

Because he's egg-greeable.

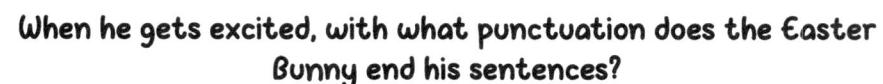

When he gets excited, with what punctuation does the Easter Bunny end his sentences?

"An eggs-claimation mark."

What does the Easter Bunny do when he inspects the eggs closely?

He "eggs-amines the eggs."

What does the Easter Bunny call the door leading outside?

"The eggs-it."

What does the Easter Bunny call someone who is really smart?

An eggs-pert.

What does the Easter Bunny call leftover eggs?

"Eggs-tras."

What does the Easter Bunny call going to a jog?

"Eggs-ercise."

What does the Easter Bunny
call people who search out new lands?

"Eggs-plorers."

What does the Easter Bunny
say instead of, "I'm tired"?

"I'm eggs-hausted."

What makes a loud booming sound,
according to the Easter Bunny?

"An eggs-plosion."

How well would the Easter Bunny say
that you did you do if you got all these questions?

"Eggs-tremely well."

CHAPTER 3
CHOCOLATE BUNNIES, EASTER LILIES, AND EASTER EGGS

Chocolate Bunnies

Did you hear about the chocolate
Easter Bunny that did crazy things?

People say he's a little nutty.

Why can you trust Easter chocolate to keep a secret,
but you cannot trust Easter marshmallows to keep a secret?

Easter chocolate doesn't make a peep.

What did the girl say as she handed her friend
the tallest piece of chocolate bunny?

" 'ere's to you."

What did the chocolate bunny say
when the bully tried to trick it?

"I ain't no sucker."

What did the chocolate bunny mutter
when it was being wrapped in aluminum?

"Foiled again!"

What happened when the boy offered
his competitor some chocolate bunny?

They each had a peace of chocolate bunny.

Why did the chocolate rabbit
open a bank account?

It was very rich.

What happened when
the chocolate bunny got angry?

It had a meltdown.

Why do Easter chocolate rabbits
taste so good?

They are choc-full of taste.

What did the chocolate bunny
say to the female chocolate bunny?

"You're sweet."

What did the chocolate bunny sigh as
the girl bit into his ear?

"Ear today; gone tomorrow."

What did the boy chocolate rabbit
say to the girl chocolate rabbit?

"You're making my heart melt."

Why was
the chocolate rabbit so sad?

He felt hollow inside.

Why can't you trust
a chocolate rabbit?

They fudge the truth.

Which chocolate rabbits
are the most relaxed?

Those that are mallow.

Why did the girl put
a chocolate bunny under her pillow?

She wanted sweet dreams.

What did the chocolate rabbit say to
the other chocolate rabbit who was sunbathing?

"You're a hot mess."

What do you call
a stolen fudge rabbit?

Hot chocolate.

What did the romantic
chocolate rabbit say to the girl?

"I'll melt in your hands."

Easter Lily

What did one young Easter Lily
say to the other?

"Let's be buds."

How is the Easter Bunny building
a new factory like a transplanted Easter Lily?

Both are putting down roots.

How is the letter A
like an Easter lily?

A bee follows both of them.

Eggs

Why can't you tell
an egg a secret?

It will crack under pressure.

Why do eggs hide?

They're a little chicken.

How did the egg call its friend?

On a shell-phone.

What's an egg's favorite sport?

Sprinting: haven't you heard that eggs tend to run a lot?

How do you describe an egg the fox
has stolen from the henhouse?

A poached egg.

How did the eggs
get on the honor roll?

They were grade A.

Which eggs are psychic?

The medium eggs.

Were the hen's eggs perfect?

They were to dye for.

Should you question what somebody is doing
if you catch the person drawing on their Easter egg?

Yes, it is sketchy behavior.

Is it easy to find
uncooked Easter eggs?

They aren't hard.

Why is looking at beautiful
Easter eggs so relaxing?

They are a master peace.

What happened when the eggs
and bacon walked into a restaurant?

The hostess said, "I'm sorry, but we don't serve breakfast here."

How did the teacher describe
Junior egg's behavior?

"He's a good egg."

Why is Easter egg hunting risky?

You put all your eggs in one basket.

**How is a lawn on Easter morning
like a video game?**

Easter eggs are everywhere.

**What happened when the boy
fell face-first onto an unboiled Easter egg?**

He had egg on his face.

**In what metropolitan area
do Easter eggs live?**

New Yolk City.

**What's the opposite of
an Easter egg?**

A Wester egg.

**What happens if more people
make traditional Easter eggs this year than last year?**

Making Easter eggs will still be a dying art.

**What happens if you throw
an Easter egg full-force at a cockroach?**

The bug is eggs terminated.

Where will the Easter egg be hidden?

It will be in the last place you think to look.
Once you find it, you won't look anywhere else.

Why does an Easter Egg Hunt have only two roles - find eggs or prepare eggs?

It's do or dye.

What did the Easter Bunny say when asked if he'd consider using non-boiled eggs?

"I might whisk it."

What do you call two close friends who eat Easter eggs?

Taste buds.

Why was the girl so embarrassed after swallowing food coloring?

She felt like she dyed a little inside.

Why was the girl sad after she drank the food coloring?

She was blue inside.

What is an original painting on an Easter egg called?

A pigment of the imagination.

Was the egg mad?

It was boiling.

Are hard-boiled eggs
the best Easter eggs?

They are hard to beat.

Why are there so few well-done eggs
found on Easter morning?

Good eggs are hard to find.

Is it exciting watching
egg dye dry?

It's as exciting as watching paint dry.

What did the dye say
to the Easter egg?

"Relax; I've got you covered."

Why was the striped egg
so hard to find?

Because it wasn't spotted.

How do you prepare to paint eggs?

You brush up.

What did the paintbrush
say to the egg?

"This may tickle a little."

66

Why did the Easter Bunny
lock the gym?

He didn't want any of his paint to run.

What did Mom say when she wanted
Junior's help peeling Easter eggs?

"Let's get cracking."

How did the boy feel when he came across
a hard chunk of something in his egg salad sandwich?

He was shell-shocked.

What did the scared child say when his mother
asked him to dip the egg in the food coloring?

"I'm too young to dye."

How did the detective
know the girl had dyed the egg?

He caught her red-handed.

CHAPTER 4
HOT-CROSS BUNS
AND
JELLY BEANS

Why did the hot cross bun
flatter its friend?

It wanted to butter him up.

What was wrong with the blown-up photo
of the hot cross bun?

The bun looked grainy.

How do you best describe a hot cross bun
that has been raised properly?

Well, bread.

Why is the inventor of
the biscuit honored?

He made a great roll model.

Which musical scale note is
the hot-cross bun's favorite?

"Dough."

Why did the boy place the dinner
roll on his knee on Easter Day?

He wanted an Easter bun knee.

Why did the boy place a stone
beside his hot cross bun?

He wanted rock-and-roll.

What is an inventory of
hot cross buns known as?

A roll call.

Why do people relax eating
hot cross buns?

It's fun to loaf.

What should you say
when you are about to eat a hot cross bun?

"Bun appetite."

What type of hotel is
most likely to serve hot cross buns?

A bread-and-breakfast.

What did Dad pun as
he stood on a hot cross bun?

"Look, everybody. I'm on a roll."

Was the hot cross bun's
baker rich?

He was rolling in the dough.

What did the hot cross bun become
when the artist drew its picture?

A roll model.

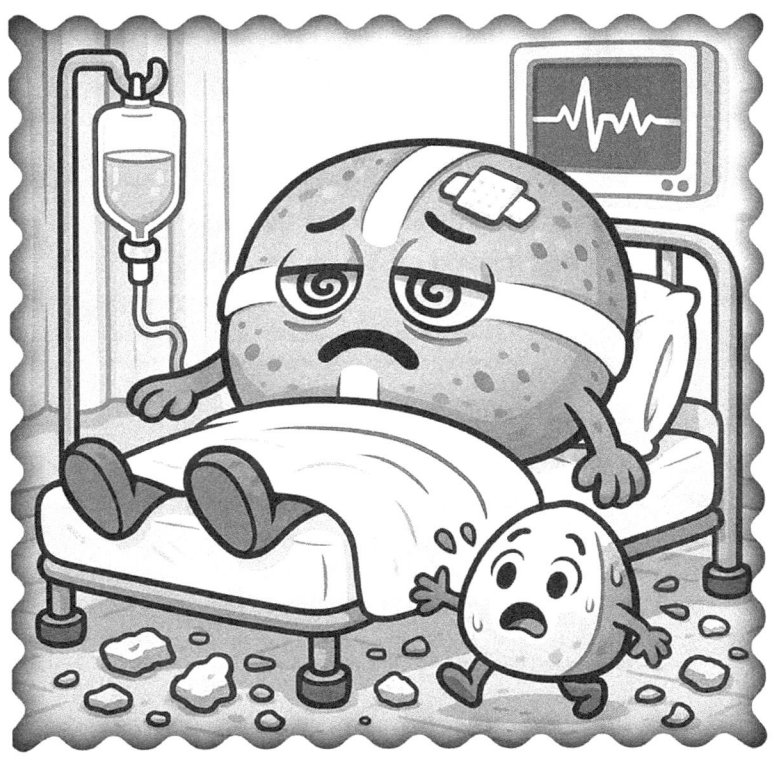

How did the hot cross bun
know he was ill?

He was feeling crumby.

What did the hot cross bun say to his girlfriend
when he broke up with her?

"You deserve butter."

When the hot cross buns were in the oven,
what did they say to motivate each other?

"Together, we rise."

What did the hot cross bun say to
his girlfriend on Valentine's Day?

"You're the only bun for me."

Why did the hot-cross-bun-eating boy say
when asked if he was having fun at the dinner table?

"No, I'm having lots of bun."

What did people yell as the hot cross bun
waved goodbye from the cruise ship?

"Bun voyage."

Why does the Easter Bunny
make hot-cross buns from scratch?

He kneads to relax.

What happened when the air conditioner broke
at the Easter Bunny's paint factory?

There were a lot of hot cross buns.

Jellybeans

How did the jellybean
describe her Easter?

"It's bean wonderful."

What kind of beans does
the Easter Rabbit grow in his garden?

Jellybeans.

What mishap did the gossip have
with her Easter basket?

She spilled the (jelly)beans.

Do jellybeans like Easter?

They have a soft spot.

What did the jellybean pack
for its vacation?

A bean bag.

How do you describe
a covering of jellybeans?

"Bean here. Bean there. Been everywhere."

CHAPTER 5
EASTER BASKETS, LENT, AND PLASTIC GRASS

Easter Baskets

Why does the Easter Bunny
put cellophane over the basket?

He wanted to wrap up the project.

What did the egg say to the basket as it
was placed inside the basket?

"I'm just along for the ride."

Was the Easter basket confident
it could hold all the eggs?

It thought it could "handle" them.

What do you call
an empty Easter basket?

A bad hare day

Why was the Easter basket sad?

It felt empty inside.

What happened when
the Easter basket got excited?

It got carried away.

What is a list that reads "basket, basket, basket, basket,
basket, basket, basket, basket, basket, and basket"?

The Easter Bunny's bucket list.

What did the basket-maker say
when his assistant told him that she was tired?

"Weave only just begun."

❋ Jokes about Easter Jokes ❋

Why aren't Easter jokes
always original?

Some are Lent.

Why shouldn't you
tell Easter jokes to eggs?

They'll crack up.

Why are jokes about
the Easter Rabbit so popular?

They are very bunny.

Lent

How is someone who gives up driving and wears rollerblades for the Easter season like a machine that gathers fuzz from black pants?

Both are Lent rollers.

Why was the carpenter sad?

He gave up his vises for Lent.

Why can't you trust restaurant owners during Lent?

Most have very fishy menus, especially on Fridays.

What is the belly button's favorite part of the Easter season?

Lent.

Why did the Easter egg behave so well during Lent?

It didn't want to get into hot water.

Plastic Grass

Why was the plastic Easter grass
so self-confident?

It knew it wasn't going to get walked on.

Why don't more people have their lawns covered
in plastic Easter grass?

Real grass will grow on you.

What did they call the contest between
the real grass and the plastic grass?

A turf war.

Which has been around longer,
real grass or plastic grass?

Real grass has roots; plastic grass does not.

Why did
the artificial grass feel sad?

He kept comparing himself to greener pastures.

How long has
artificial grass existed?

For a lawn time.

What happened when
the plastic grass was carried off?

It was lawn gone.

When the artificial grass wasn't damp, and he wanted it to have a touch of morning moisture, what did the Easter Bunny have to do?

Make dew.

CHAPTER 6
EASTER KNOCK-KNOCK JOKES

Knock-Knock jokes may be eggs-actly what you need to make the mood festive. As the joke teller, you will read the first line. To help you keep your place, your lines are in bold. The other person will simply say, "Who's there?" and, having heard your answer, will seek clarification. You will then share the punny answer. Most people know the format of a knock-knock joke and will not need to read their lines.

Knock-Knock.
Who's there?
Ima Reilly.
Ima Reilly, who?
Ima Reilly big fan of Easter knock-knock jokes.

Knock-Knock.
Who's there?
Shelley Hans.
Shelley Hans, who?
Shelly Hans is what you will get if you peel Easter eggs.

Knock-Knock.
Who's there?
Hyde.
Hyde who?
Hyde the Easter eggs, and I'll try to find them.

Knock-Knock.
Who's there?
Phil D. Basket.
Phil D. Basket, who?
Phil D. Basket with candy and Easter eggs, please.

Knock-Knock.
Who's there?
Easter.
Easter who?
Easter (eased her) mind when I said Easter morning was going to be free of rain.

Knock-Knock.
Who's there?
Dye It.
Dye It, who?
Dye It is something I need to go on if I am going to lose weight.

Knock-Knock.
Who's there?
Rabbit.
Rabbit who?
Rabbit up in there; other people need a turn, too.

Knock-Knock.
Who's there?
Holly Days.
Holly Days, who?
Holly Days like Easter make me giddy.

Knock-Knock.
Who's there?
X.
X who?
X (eggs) are fun to find on Easter.

Knock-Knock.
Who's there?
Cottontail.
Cottontail who?
Cottontail what you were saying; can you say it again, please?

Knock-Knock.
Who's there?
Todd.
Todd who?
Todd some pretty good Easter jokes, haven't we?

Knock-Knock.
Who's there?
Pole Tree.
Pole Tree, who?
Pole Tree are needed if there are going to be eggs.

Knock-Knock.
Who's there?
Eggs.
Eggs who?
**Eggs and pains are a part of running around looking
for Easter eggs.**

Knock-Knock.
Who's there?
Four Eggs.
Four Eggs, who?
**Four Eggs-ample (for example), I think you are good
at telling knock-knock jokes.**

Knock-Knock.
Who's there?
Heidi.
Heidi who?
**Heidi eggs really well so it takes me a while to find
them.**

Knock-Knock.
Who's there?
Eggs Aisle.
Eggs Aisle, who?
Eggs Aisle occurs when one is barred from one's native country.

Knock-Knock.
Who's there?
Hare Say.
Hare Say who?
Hare Say is things you have heard but have not been proven as true; they are rumors.

Knock-Knock.
Who's there?
Eggs Sighted.
Eggs Sighted who?
Eggs Sighted to go on an Easter egg hunt.

Knock-Knock.
Who's there?
Gene Eric.
Gene Eric, who?
Gene Eric eggs are boring to me; I like mine dyed and covered in stickers.

Knock-Knock.
Who's there?
Hyden.
Hyden who?
Hyden my Easter candy, so you can't find it.

Knock-Knock.
Who's there?
Eggs Plain.
Eggs Plain, who?
Eggs Plain to me when the Easter Bunny is expected to come.

Knock-Knock.
Who's there?
Eggs Act.
Eggs Act who?
Eggs Act day of Easter varies from year to year.

Knock-Knock.
Who's there?
Earl Lee.
Earl Lee, who?
Earl Lee risers get to see the Easter sun come up.

Knock-Knock.
Who's there?
Bunny Fits.
Bunny fits who?
Bunny fits (benefits) of an indoor egg hunt include not getting wet if it rains and no bugs crawling on the eggs.

Knock-Knock.
Who's there?
Dye? No, sir.
Dye? No, sir, who?
Dye? No, sir, goes r-r-r-r-r-r-r-r-r-roar!

Knock-Knock.
Who's there?
Marty Graw.
Marty Graw who?
Marty Graw is the carnival before Lent.

Knock-Knock.
Who's there?
Eggs Sighted.
Eggs Sighted who?
Eggs Sighted about going on an Easter egg hunt.

Knock-Knock.
Who's there?
Diego.
Diego who?
Diego in the Easter basket.

Knock-Knock.
Who's there?
One Two.
One Two who?
One Two tell some more knock-knock Easter jokes.

Knock-Knock.
Who's there?
Hare.
Hare who?
Hare we go, telling more good jokes.

Knock-Knock.
Who's there?
Hare.
Hare who?
Hare-larious jokes we are telling.

Knock-Knock.
Who's there?
Hare.
Hare who?
Hare what I have to say – Happy Easter!

DID YOU ENJOY THE BOOK?

If you did, we are ecstatic. If not, please write your complaint to us and we will ensure we fix it.

If you're feeling generous, there is something important that you can help me with – tell other people that you enjoyed the book.

Ask a grown-up to write about it on Amazon. When they do, more people will find out about the book. It also lets Amazon know that we are making kids around the world laugh. Even a few words and ratings would go a long way.

If you have any ideas or jokes that you think are super funny, please let us know. We would love to hear from you. Our email address is -

riddleland@riddlelandforkids.com

ABOUT RIDDLELAND

Riddleland is a mum + dad run publishing company. We are passionate about creating fun and innovative books to help children develop their reading skills and fall in love with reading. If you have suggestions for us or want to work with us, shoot us an email at riddleland@riddlelandforkids.com Our family's favorite quote:

"Creativity is an area in which younger people have a tremendous advantage since they have an endearing habit of always questioning past wisdom and authority."

~ Bill Hewlett

www.ingramcontent.com/pod-product-compliance
Lightning Source LLC
Chambersburg PA
CBHW061705120626
46550CB00003B/1098